UNLEASH THE
LEADER WITHIN
ACHIEVE YOUR TRUE POTENTIAL

Wallace H. Bailey

ISBN-10: 0-692-90933-8
ISBN-13: 978-0692-90933-1

For quantity purchases of this book contact:
talktome@coachwallace.com

Published by:

Gator Family Brazilian Jiu-Jitsu LLC

Deland, Fl. 32720

Edited by:

Drew King

Printed in the United States of America

"YOU CAN HAVE EVERYTHING IN LIFE THAT YOU WANT, IF YOU WILL JUST HELP ENOUGH OTHER PEOPLE GET WHAT THEY WANT."

ZIG ZIGLAR

Table of Contents

At the end of every chapter you will find a question and blank pages to write your answers. The focus is to bring attention to specific details of personal growth. This is an amazing discovery tool that can be used to help you *Unleash The Leader Within*!

ACKNOWLEDGMENTS

To my beautiful wife LeeAnn. My dog C. Katie Run, Lil'
Mama and my entire family for your unending support.
Thank you!

INTRODUCTION

In 1981, I was ten years old and my favorite
thing to do in the whole wide world was to
play baseball. I played on a team called the
Pierson Twins sponsored by the local Lions
club. We were the best little league team in
all of Volusia County. We went thirty-zero,
winning every single game we played. We had
some real superstars on our team. One of
them even went on to play in the major
leagues. Chipper Jones played third base for
the Atlanta Braves.

I was pretty good, but I also had anxiety.
Not the butterflies in the stomach, lump in
the throat kind, but gut-wrenching I'm-going-
to-pass-out kind of anxiety. I would drink
antacid before every game. It didn't really
help with the anxiety but it did keep me from
throwing up. Before I'd get up to bat I was
nervous about missing the ball. I would blink
really fast and get it out of the way, so that I
could have my eyes open when the ball came.
One day, as he always did, my grandpa asked

how I was doing so I explained all the anxiety I was having. He put his arm around me, pulled me in close, and smiled as he said, "I won't always be here so I want you to know. There's a leader inside you that you have to let show. It's just under the surface, it's just under the skin. You can do it, I promise, just unleash the leader within!"

The next Saturday there was a big game. I asked my mom and dad if I could ride my bicycle to the game. It was a long way from our house to the ballpark. About halfway there I had a decision to make. I could ride along the road around a large pasture. Or I could take a shortcut straight through the pasture and save a lot of time. There was one big problem. There was a really big bull in that pasture. I felt the anxiety creeping in. I thought to myself, "I can do this, I got this!" Take the bull by the horns so to speak and conquer my fears. I threw my bicycle over the fence, climbed over myself and took off. I never looked back. I played my heart out that day. I threw two people out, caught a fly ball, and even hit a double. My mom picked me up after the game.

We drove home and as we pulled into the driveway, my mom broke the news to me. My grandpa had passed. My eyes filled with tears and, as my heart began to break, it hit me like a ton of bricks right on my chest. Just when I needed him the most. I remembered those words my grandpa had spoke to me.

"I won't always be here so I want you to know. There's a leader inside you that you have to let show. It's just under the surface, it's just under the skin. You can do it I promise, just unleash the leader within!"

CHAPTER 1

Learn the #1 Asset of a Leader and How To Get More of It

I was having lunch with a friend one day and he was telling me that some time ago he wanted to start exercising. He went on to say that he looked around at all of the gyms nearby to find a place to start working out.

He called a few of them, got prices, and even visited some of them to get a vibe of the place. Stating that he finally decided on a gym to go to, got out his calendar and started planning the days to attend. To make his goal very clear, he wrote it all down.

I told him that was a great plan and asked how it was going. He looked at me very sadly and continued his story. He said a few days passed, then even a few weeks, and decided that he just couldn't make it to the gym. So he decided it would be better to get a small home gym for convenience. He said he had researched thousands of pieces of equipment and purchased a good one. Bringing it home, he exclaimed that this time he was serious. Once again, he got out his calendar and a red pen, and marked down his exercise days, even going online and downloading a whole bunch of exercise routines.

When he had finished explaining everything that he had done to start exercising, I asked him how that was working out. Again, he got that same sad look on his face that he had before. He looked down at his half-eaten sandwich, then back at me and answered, "it's the same outcome as before."

I asked him, "what the heck happened?"

He looked me straight in the face and told me he was so excited and so enthused to start working out. He went through the whole process and planned everything out, even spending his hard-earned money on equipment. I looked him back square in the face and said, "I can tell you just exactly what happened. Your plan is working you. You're working so hard on your plan that you forgot the one important factor. The one thing to make it all work. It's one of those terrible four letter words. It's called WORK." I explained that his plan was working him instead of the other way around.

Does this scenario sound familiar? Go ahead and put whatever goal you've been trying to achieve into this situation. The chances are extremely high that you haven't met your goal because your plan has been working you. Taking up all of your time and driving you crazy. At some point you must hit the pavement. The rubber must meet the road and get traction. Pick up the phone and call somebody to hold you accountable. Be committed to doing whatever it takes to succeed. The best laid plans mean absolutely nothing if no action is taken. In case you've forgotten, I've looked up the word "work" for you, and the definition is below.

Definition of work ***(Merriam-Webster)

1

: activity in which one exerts strength or faculties to do or perform something:

a : sustained physical or mental effort to overcome obstacles and achieve an objective or result

b : the labor, task, or duty that is one's accustomed means of livelihood

c : a specific task, duty, function, or assignment often being a part or phase of some larger activity

2

a : energy expended by natural phenomena

b : the result of such energy <sand dunes are the work of sea and wind>

c : the transference of energy that is produced by the motion of the point of application of a force and is measured by multiplying the force and the displacement of its point of application in the line of action

3

a : something that results from a particular manner or method of working, operating, or devising <careful police work> <clever camera work>

I've read this definition numerous times and I still cannot find the words "someday," "tomorrow," "when," or "if this happens" or "if that happens"! You *must* put in the work. Working on a goal or problem means taking action on the things that really matter. The things that will really get you closer to your goal. After you've done all of the research and made your plan, you *have* to start working.

I was just working on my website yet again. I never think it's *good enough*. I'm staring at the screen and I started asking myself questions. "Why am I doing this? What is my main objective for this site?" Then it hit me like a ton of bricks. Like a freight train coming at full speed. "I'm doing this to get booked for speaking engagements!" But it will only work if people come to the site. "What if I reached out to people I wanted to work with directly?" I thought. What a novel idea! I've heard it said and read it thousands of times. Hell, I've even wrote it hundreds of times. It's the phrase *"Take Action."* Yes, I know, I know. I got caught up again in trying to reinvent the wheel.

I immediately logged out of my site. I looked up the exact people and organizations at my local university that my message is perfect for. I then found the people in charge of those programs and sent them a personal email. I sent ten emails including a link to my website. Within an hour I had received two replies from people that were interested in working together. I could have *took action* continuing to work on my website for that hour. Where would I be? Still hoping people found the site.

The lesson here is *take action* on what gets results. Being busy and working hard on the wrong things will only lead to frustration. You know what's really funny? I checked the analytics for my site. Want to know how many of those email recipients clicked the link to my website? This is hilarious, zero! That's right, absolutely no one even visited anyway. Be sure to focus on what gets results. Do not get caught up staying busy and working hard on things that aren't getting the job done.

If you want a raise or promotion where you work, just doing a great job is not enough. You already get paid for that. You must let

the boss know what you want and ask
specific questions on what is expected of you
to meet your objective.

Getting to where you want to be requires
work. You must *take action*! But beware, take
the *action* that gets results. That's how we
start working our plan to unleash the leader
within.

WHAT ACTION CAN I TAKE RIGHT NOW THAT WILL GET ME CLOSER TO MY GOAL?

_____

_____

_____

_____

_____

_____

_____

_____

_____

_____

_____

_____

_____

_____

_____

_____

_____

_____

_____

_____

_____

_____

CHAPTER 2

Self-Image (Confidence) is the Key

Being able to see yourself as a leader or even being good at something can be a very hard thing to do. When I was a kid, and still today, I'm usually the shortest person in the room. Does it bother me? Not at all. I guess when I was really young I just accepted it, because in reality there's absolutely nothing I can do about it anyway. I could dwell on the fact that I'm short but the only person it would hurt would be myself. No one else seems to really care. Are there challenges? Well, of course there are. Everyone has some sort of challenge in everyday life, don't they? Everyone has their strengths and weaknesses. Each one of us are unique in our own special way but it is our strengths, our talents, that are the very essence of our personalities. We hide our weaknesses so that no one ever see's that part of us. Why on earth do we do that? We care too much about what other people think of us.

How you see yourself, your self-image is key. It must never be about someone else's opinion of you. Everyone is entitled to their own opinion, but as a matter of fact, it's just that, an opinion. You know yourself better than anyone. Your opinion of yourself must be positive and rock solid if you want to unleash the leader within.

Let's begin with your strengths. Your specific set of talents are what make you unique. There is a precise and direct connection between your talents and your accomplishments in your life so far. What characteristics or traits do you feel are your strongest? Can you make people laugh? Can you multitask? Are you persistent? Think of your success so far as a straight line. Up until this very point it has been on a slow gradual incline. Keep doing the same things and that line will still gradually go up over a long period of time. It may very well level off. Make a list of what you feel are your strengths. Not what others may think but what you believe are your best qualities. Take your time and really think about it. There may be certain things you are extremely good at but don't necessarily recognize right away because they're second nature.

Now let's turn to your weaknesses. Your weaknesses are where the gold is. Wait, what? You may be asking yourself, "did I read that right?" Yes, you read it correctly! Your weaknesses are exactly where the leader within you is hiding. Your innate talents and learned abilities that you have right now have brought you to where you are. Keep doing the same thing and keep getting the same results, right? In order to progress and get different and even better results, we must look at the characteristics and traits that are not our strong suits. These are in fact the exact barriers that will keep you from where you want to be. Think about it this way. You've made it this far on all of your strengths. Your job, your career, your life has been built solidly on your strengths alone. Think of that gradual incline of success again. Working diligently on your weaknesses will make that line jump straight up exponentially. That's what we want.

Learning something new and different can be challenging to say the least. I know, I've seen it time and time again. At my Brazilian Jiu-Jitsu Academy, kids and adults come in and try to do basic drills, movements, and techniques. It's very difficult at first because they've never done it before. All of the drills have weird names and feel really strange yet everyone else seems to be proficient at them because they've put in the work to learn them, making the new student feel out of place. There, my friend, is the secret. Did you see it? The secret to developing unstoppable confidence. The kind of self-image that great leaders have!

"WORK"

There it is again. That dirty little four letter word. Let me drive home the importance of working on your weaknesses.

One day a young kid started Jiu-Jitsu at our Academy. He was very smart and intelligent. He had excellent manners and a supreme attitude. He had all of the building blocks of a leader. Something was missing. What he lacked was rock solid confidence. His self-image was not up to par, even though he had every other quality needed to be a great leader. He came to every class within the last year. At first, he was shy about grappling with kids bigger than him but he didn't give up. He'd get beat and come back for more. I watched as he focused on the techniques I would teach class after class. His grappling became better. He started to win a few more matches. As he began to win more, his confidence grew. His self-image was growing. What was his secret? What helped him grow his self-image? He worked on his weaknesses. His new found confidence, coupled with his already amazing talents, catapulted him to new heights. I am proud to say he earned the 2016 Warrior Spirit Award for our Academy.

Start today and try something you have never done before. Something that might scare you a little. Take baby steps, stick with it, and watch your confidence soar.

By doing small things consistently we really won't notice much progress, but over time those small consistent actions add up to a mountain. All of a sudden we have accomplished more than we ever thought possible.

Take a big of a step as you can but start today. Start right now. You can do it, I promise. Unleash the leader within.

WHAT ACTION OR STEPS CAN I TAKE RIGHT NOW OR IN THE NEAR FUTURE TO BUILD MY SELF CONFIDENCE?

_____

_____

_____

_____

_____

_____

_____

_____

_____

_____

_____

_____

_____

_____

_____

_____

_____

_____

_____

_____

_____

_____

_____

_____

CHAPTER 3

How Your Attitude Determines Your Altitude

Several months ago I had a meeting planned with someone that took a lot of correspondence and coordinating to get. The person I was going to meet with had a very busy schedule and thankfully fit me in. I arrived at his office twenty minutes early fully prepared. The receptionist cheerfully greeted me and started explaining that my name was not on the schedule for that day. I politely asked her if I was scheduled for another day, that maybe I had gotten the days confused. As she typed away on her computer I felt a flood of emotions consume me. At first I felt angry at the receptionist because she had given me information I did not expect or like. That feeling quickly turned to disappointment at the thought of the meeting I had fully expected to happen would not.

The receptionist turned back to me after checking her calendar and told me that she did not find my name anywhere on the books. It was here that I almost lost it. Notice the key word there, *almost*. I had corresponded with the guy I was supposed to be meeting with for weeks. We had agreed upon a time and a place. My schedule for the next few weeks was already booked solid. I was fully expecting to meet with him today. I could've let that lady have it and gave her a real piece of my mind. I *could have*!

I took a deep breath, reached into my pocket, and pulled out my cell phone. I opened the last email I had received regarding our meeting. I smiled and showed it to the receptionist. After reading it she picked up the phone and spoke with someone. When she was done she looked at me, smiled, and stated I could go in now, that the gentleman I was meeting was looking forward to seeing me. As I walked into his office, he apologized for the confusion. Apparently he had forgotten to copy his receptionist on our email correspondence so she was totally unaware.

Has anything like this ever happened to you? Did you lose it? If you did, how did that turn out for you? Did it make things better? In this particular situation, if I had gone off on the receptionist, do you think I would have had a snowball's chance at ever getting the meeting that day or any other day for that matter?

Attitude meant everything in this situation! Every day in every situation we have a choice. The choice to respond and the choice to react. That choice sits squarely on your shoulders and no one else's. Did I feel angry at first? You bet I did! The choice I made was to respond to the situation rather than the person, keeping my attitude in check. Had I reacted and yelled at the person giving me news I didn't like or agree with, I would have made the situation a lot worse. Even jeopardizing my chances for a meeting at all.

Being a leader that people trust means having a positive attitude as well. How many people in a leadership position do you know just fly off the handle for no reason? I'm sure your answer is "not very many." Especially trusted people of authority. If they do, the chances are that they won't be there much longer.

Decisions, decisions, so what's it going to be? React or respond to every situation? If you truly want to unleash the leader within you'll have to respond to situations rather than react to them. People will continually push your buttons every day. Trust me, there are always going to be *those* people. The fact is you control those buttons and what they do when they are pushed.

Your attitude is in direct response to your immediate feelings. It doesn't have to be that way. You can have a positive attitude one hundred percent of the time every second of the day. It all rests squarely on your shoulders.

Bad things happen to good people. It's just a matter of fact. No matter what you do or think bad things just happen. It's a part of life. When bad things happen it's very important to remember that things will not always be this way, they are always temporary. When these things happen, just repeat this phrase:

"This situation is only temporary.

WHAT ACTION OR STEPS CAN I TAKE RIGHT NOW TO HAVE A BETTER ATTITUDE WITH MYSELF AND OTHERS?

_____

_____

_____

_____

_____

_____

_____

_____

_____

_____

_____

_____

_____

_____

_____

_____

_____

_____

_____

_____

_____

CHAPTER 4

Don't Just Go Through Life, Grow Through Life

Years ago when I was in my twenties, I lived in West Palm Beach, Florida. I had a job at an engineering firm that specialized in concrete restoration. The job itself was fairly simple. Go out to various construction sites, that were often times on the beach, and inspect the work that was going on and ensure the work was done properly. I would then go back to the office, copy and paste the previous day's report and change the date. Like I said, fairly simple. One day the manager invited me to do an initial inspection for a potential new client. It was a straight forward inspection, and I took a ton of notes and pictures. When we arrived back at the office my manager told me he was going home and to have a report on his desk by the next morning. "Yes, sir!" I told him.

Instead of the same boring copy and paste, I decided to show him what I could do. The report took me the entire rest of the day to complete. I checked it several times for errors, and as I laid it on his desk I thought to myself, "wow, he is going to be so impressed with this masterpiece." As I walked into work the next morning, there was a spring in my step. When I sat down at my desk I could immediately tell that the IT guy had been in overnight to clean up the computer systems. It was obvious by the screen saver he would always display: "You must comply." I was shaking my head as I heard, "Wallace, get in here!" through the closed door of my manager's office.

I opened the door and walked into his office with a huge smile on my face. "Sit down," he said while holding the report. "Didn't I tell you to have a report of the inspection we did yesterday on my desk this morning?" he said while never looking up.

"Yes, sir!" I replied.

He looked up at me and slid the paper in front of me. "What is this?" he asked with a disgusted look. I explained it was my report. He went on to tell me how disappointed he was with me and that however creative the document I gave him was, it was certainly not what he wanted. I sat there in shock as he continued to explain the procedures that were to be followed. After what seemed like an hour and after he finished his tirade, I calmly stated that I believed we were now on the same page. "Same page?" he sneered. "We aren't even in the same library!" he added.

"The right parking lot maybe?" I asked. He looked right through me, pointing to the door. I picked up my masterpiece, walked to my desk and began to copy and paste. Five minutes later I walked back into his office and handed him the new report. He was ecstatic, like nothing ever happened. I put in my notice not long after that.

How could I possibly work some place where my creativity was not appreciated? How can we grow professionally or even as a person when there is no opportunity to be challenged? How can we unleash the leader within when there is no opportunity to take the lead?

The job I got the next week proved much better. I signed on with an underground utility company. I worked hard and was able to show my true abilities. It was only about six months later I was offered a manager's position. I accepted with the condition that I would be able to use my creativity, think outside the box, and get the job done even if it did not follow general standards. They gave me my wish. I saved the company a ton of money and time over the next year. I think to this day they still use some of my ideas.

It's time to get out of your box. Leaders have a vision of things that most people don't see. If you have an idea go for it. Make it known.

Don't just go through life, grow through it!

WHAT ACTIONS CAN I TAKE RIGHT NOW TO EXPRESS MY CREATIVITY?

_____

_____

_____

_____

_____

_____

_____

_____

_____

_____

_____

_____

_____

_____

_____

_____

_____

_____

_____

_____

_____

_____

CHAPTER 5

Lasting Change

We all have areas of our life that could stand a little improvement. We tend to try little things here and there to make things better. What generally ends up happening is we don't follow through, and we end up doing the same things over and over. We become so comfortable doing these things, even if it's not helping us at all. Even if they're actually hurting us.

If you really want real and lasting change, here's a simple checklist to get you started on the path to success.

Belief

For a very real and lasting change in our lives, we must truly believe without a shadow of a doubt, and through no uncertain terms, that we can and will change whatever it is that is keeping us from success. Keeping a positive mental attitude through change is imperative to your self-belief and confidence.

Believing in yourself is up to you and you alone. Think back to all of the struggles and challenges you have had in your life up to now, no matter what they were. You have overcome every single one of them. Now think back on all the great accomplishments you have achieved. They make you feel great right? Now take that feeling that you have right now and build on it. Believe!

Absolute Commitment

My friend and fellow Toastmaster, Rose Schumacher, gave an amazing presentation on this subject. She used the brilliant analogy of ham and eggs.

She emphasized, while the chicken was involved, the pig was fully committed. While being involved is something very commendable, taking your commitment all the way shows your true determination.

There is a very clear and distinct difference in being absolutely committed. Real and lasting change only happens when you put your heart and soul into it. There has to be passion. A burning desire that nothing will stop you!

Start With Only One Thing

Old habits are hard to break. Especially if there are many. Putting all of your intense focus on only one thing at a time will greatly enhance your chances of success.

Trying to multi-task with so many things pulling us in all different directions is not the route we need to take. Focusing on one small task at a time will create momentum. Building on that momentum, we can accomplish these small goals. Building confidence, and bringing us ever closer to our ultimate success. If the past is something you are finding difficult to let go, I would suggest a book called *Beyond Yesterday*, strategies to leave the past where it belongs. It's available on Amazon.

That Little Voice In Your Head

I strongly encourage you to focus on the story you tell yourself. The conversation you have in your head every second of every day. It has such a dramatic impact on your life that I devoted an entire chapter of this book on it. I've even created a course and included it as a keynote speech I present.

For this specific chapter it is of utmost importance that you remove any limiting language in the conversation you have with yourself.

Your Self-Talk is an extremely huge part of any success you will have. Be very careful what you say to yourself. Your entire future depends on it!

WHAT SPECIFIC ACTIONS OR STEPS CAN I TAKE RIGHT NOW TO ENSURE I FOLLOW THROUGH ON MY GOALS?

_____

_____

_____

_____

_____

_____

_____

_____

_____

_____

_____

_____

_____

_____

_____

_____

_____

_____

_____

_____

_____

CHAPTER 6

Focus on What Matters Most

When I was about twelve years old I was into competitive archery. My parents would take me to different events all over the state of Florida.

The objective was relatively simple. All you had to do was shoot three arrows at a target from varying distances. Some targets were your typical circles or rings on paper with corresponding values. The outer circles scored less points and the inner circles scored more. Several competitions would have trails winding through the woods and feature 3-D targets. At the end of the tournaments, the judges would tally up all of the scores and announce a winner.

I did pretty well, winning quite a few competitions. Yes, I put in a lot of the work but I can't take all of the credit. My dad deserves recognition too. He was responsible for adjusting my bow.

I used a compound bow and it had a huge difference in the traditional recurve bow. It had a complex pulley system that allowed for less draw strength (pulling it back) and more power (when you let it go.) It also had sights that you could use to aim better. That's where my dad would come in. Being able to hit your target (or goal) in anything requires intense focus. You may be able to hit your target occasionally shooting willy-nilly but it's not very effective in the long run. The following is the lesson that my dad taught me and one I still use today.

When I got my first bow it wasn't sighted correctly, so when I looked through the peephole on the string and lined up the pin with the target, the arrow would hit nowhere near where I wanted it to go. My dad told me to shoot a few more arrows, being sure to be consistent every time. I shot three arrows and they all went to lower right side of the target. They were not in a "group" or really close together but more sporadic. I handed the bow to him to adjust the sight but he handed it back to me and said, "be patient and shoot some more." I didn't understand but he assured me he would fix it after I had shot a good group. I continued to shoot another twenty arrows, finally getting a bunch in one concentrated group. My dad then adjusted the sights a little bit more, being sure to not move them too far. I shot another twenty arrows and had a tight group just outside the bullseye. He carefully adjusted the sites once more and every arrow after that was perfect.

Now let's take that lesson and apply it to our everyday lives. How many times have you tried something once and it didn't work so you tried something different? Being consistent in your approach may not move you as far as you want towards your target or goal. It will, however, give you the feedback and analytics to show you what's working and what's not. Your sight may be just off target. By only taking one shot and adjusting your sight, you may occasionally hit your target. We want to hit every shot every time. Being patient and changing one small thing, one small step at a time will pay dividends. By jumping all over the place you will never find the solution.

Be sure to give things time. Give them a chance. Shoot enough arrows to get real feedback, enough data to actually analyze. Focus on what matters most: results! Then you can weigh the positives and negatives and make an educated guess on how to move forward.

Leaders are able to lead by experience. How do they get it? By taking action and carefully analyzing the results. Then they make a small change and test again.

WHAT SMALL THINGS CAN I CHANGE RIGHT NOW THAT WILL MAKE THE GREATEST IMPACT ON MY LIFE?

_____

_____

_____

_____

_____

_____

_____

_____

_____

_____

_____

_____

_____

_____

_____

_____

_____

_____

_____

_____

_____

_____

_____

CHAPTER 7

The One Thing All Leaders Use to Their Advantage

I was having a conversation the other day with an associate of mine in a corner booth at a restaurant. We were discussing business when a guy walked over who obviously knew the person I was having lunch with. We were introduced and after the general pleasantries, the guy asked my friend what we were working on. He politely stated we were having a private business meeting. The guy started telling us all about a new business he was working on. He went on and on *and on,* I thought he would never quit. I don't think he stopped to take a breath. When he finally paused for a brief second, I cut in and told him it was nice meeting him and that I only had a few minutes left to finish lunch. He started again, this time talking about how time flies and we never seem to have enough of it.

Does this ever happen to you? Probably way too often right? Here's the thing. People listen to reply, rather than listen to understand and respond. It's okay, it's basic human nature to want to participate in a conversation. We want to sound interested and interesting, and reply with a similar story or one-up the other person with one of our own that relates to what we just heard. It's very true that people like to talk about themselves.

The one thing that leaders use to their advantage is listening. Not to reply but to truly understand what the other person is trying to convey, their true message.

There are so many things that go on in an ordinary conversation. Studies have shown that body language says more than the actual words that are spoken.

I would love to get into all the aspects of body language but that would be an entirely different book, and so many great minds have already done that. I do want to cover several tactics that can help you achieve your true potential and unleash the leader within.

Listening is an advantage that all leaders use. The non-verbal part of communication plays a key role in how we can and should respond. When someone says something to you and their body language contradicts it or is telling you something different, we must analyze the true meaning behind what we've seen and heard. If someone says, "I really want to help you out tomorrow," but has his hands are folded and looking at the ground when speaking, the chances of him really meaning what he said are pretty low.

The tone of someone's voice also plays a vital role in really learning what they are trying to say. When someone's voice is loud and bold, we can probably discern that they are confident or upset. On the flip side, we can learn if someone is bashful or ashamed if they are speaking in a soft voice. Try to look, listen, and really understand what someone is trying to say before responding to them.

It's important as a leader to keep a calm and steady tone in our voices. We must remain patient. Be confident with your words and your body language. Walk with authority, with your chin up and shoulders back. Exude confidence in the face of adversity and really listen to what others have to say.

Being assertive is another key aspect of leaders. Notice in the previous story how I was patient and courteous to the stranger who had butted in to our meeting. When I found an opening, when the guy finally took a breath and stopped talking for a split second, I politely stated a point. I did not offend but I did not mince words either. It is so very important to be polite but firm.

"Listen first to respond rather than reply!"

WHAT ACTION OR STEPS CAN I TAKE RIGHT NOW TO IMPROVE MY LISTENING SKILLS?

_____

_____

_____

_____

_____

_____

_____

_____

_____

_____

_____

_____

_____

_____

_____

_____

_____

_____

_____

_____

_____

_____

_____

CHAPTER 8

The Blame Game

Have you ever had a part time job at a fast food restaurant? My very first job was at Kentucky Fried Chicken cooking the Colonel's famous recipe. If you ever wanted to know the secret recipe I can tell you. It comes in a plain white pouch with small black letters that read: "eleven herbs and spices." There you have it.

I enjoyed smelling the chicken cooking and the other people that worked there were pretty cool. We all had our specific jobs and ran a tight ship. On the days we were scheduled to close, we would have different duties to shut things down for the night. On one occasion there were three of us who were closing the store. We were all ready to get the heck out of there. It had been really slow that night and the time was really dragging. Not to mention it was Friday night and I was a teenager. We knocked everything out, cleaning from top to bottom. We turned off all the cookers, machines and lights.

Or so we thought. Come to find out one of the warmers were left on and ran the electricity bill through the roof. Management was not happy at all. All three of us were called in and interrogated individually. I believe the general consensus was that it was somebody else's fault. In reality all three of us had the responsibility to ensure everything was clean and turned off.

The easiest thing to do when something doesn't go according to plan is to blame someone else. True leaders have integrity. Doing the right thing even when no one is looking. It's not very wise to hold people accountable when you yourself won't accept responsibility. If you realize you've made a mistake, be the very first person to admit it. Hold yourself accountable and own it.

Blaming others puts you in a tight spot. It's a no win situation. Right or wrong, the other person will more than likely be offended and you will be seen as the bad guy. I'd like to suggest a win-win scenario where you and the other person can benefit.

First of all, always try to focus on the action and not the person. Pointing out what someone said or did will direct attention toward the issue and the person will be less likely to feel attacked personally. Secondly, I like to ask the other person for their ideas on a resolution to the issue. Putting the ball in their court is beneficial in two ways. It makes them part of the solution and they will be more likely to follow through with a plan they create themselves. *That* is a win-win.

Blaming circumstances is another thing entirely. Constantly blaming other people or circumstances for your situation is bull. All of your complaining will accomplish nothing! Set a goal so high you can never reach it. Do your very best to reach that goal using every resource available. You will be surprised at how much you can really achieve.

Don't join in the blame game. It's a lose-lose situation.

WHAT ARE SOME WORDS, PHRASES OR QUESTIONS I CAN USE INSTEAD OF CASTING BLAME?

_____

_____

_____

_____

_____

_____

_____

_____

_____

_____

_____

_____

_____

_____

_____

_____

_____

_____

_____

_____

_____

_____

_____

_____

CHAPTER 9

Taking Personal Responsibility

I used to work for an underground utility company. One day we were putting a drainage pipe under a road. It started by cutting a wide strip of asphalt and removing it. The next phase began by removing about ten feet of dirt at a specific grade to make room for an eight foot concrete pipe. After putting the pipe in place, I would use a machine called an excavator to place dirt back on either side of the pipe to hold it in place while I set another one. About half way through the project I noticed the next pipe to go in had a crack in it. No one else had seen it or pointed it out. It wasn't real big, maybe four inches or so. The fact was that over time that small crack could let water running through the pipe saturate the ground and cause the pavement to fail. It could also get bigger or break altogether under the intense pressure of vehicles running over it day after day.

Either of those scenarios could very possibly cause accidents or even injuries. Not to mention all of the time and labor for the repairs that would be necessary. Is it possible that a small, four inch crack could cause such problems? There was a decision to be made and it was up to me. The right thing to do was obvious but that would put the project in reverse, causing lost time. We had a limited amount of time to complete the installation because we had the whole road shut down. Was it worth the potential risk?

"Do the right thing even when no one is looking."

Of course I told the hill man, the guy in charge of hooking the pipes up, to get a different one ready. There's a huge difference in getting a job done and getting a job done right.

Integrity is a prominent quality in leaders. They take personal responsibility and do the right thing even when no one is looking.

Sure, I could have just kept going and put the pipe in. No one would have ever known. Any issues that could have possibly resulted from the small crack would have taken years to develop, if anything even happened at all. But I knew and did something about it.

If you ever find yourself driving in West Palm Beach Florida and you come to the intersection of Summit Boulevard and Jog Road. You can rest assure the road will hold you.

WHAT ACTION OR STEPS CAN I TAKE RIGHT NOW TO GAIN PERSONAL RESPONSIBILTY?

_____
_____
_____
_____
_____
_____
_____
_____
_____
_____
_____
_____
_____
_____
_____
_____
_____
_____
_____
_____
_____
_____
_____
_____
_____
_____

CHAPTER 10

Expectations

I was planning to go fishing with my dad one weekend. I watched the weather the night before and the weather guy was saying there was a front coming. That's bad in one way because it means rain and I'm against fishing in the rain. (Right there with Hank Williams Jr. on that one.) In the good way, it meant fishing would be really good—a front changes the barometric pressure and the fish begin to feed. The weather man said it would start to get nasty around three o'clock. With an early start, me and my dad could get out there at a prime time to catch our limit and get back in before dinner.

I headed out early Saturday morning up to my dad's house. He was waiting as usual on me. The boat was hooked to the truck and loaded with gear. "The fish'll be done bitin' by the time we get there!" was my dad's one comment. I took that as my cue to load up in the truck. We chatted on the ride to the lake. Mostly about landmarks around the town we had lived in so long and how things have changed. We arrived at the boat ramp to find a picture perfect lake. There was no wind and no mosquitos. This was it! The calm before the storm. We idled out of the pass past the lily pads and alligators. We hit the edge of Florida's second largest lake, Lake George, and took off. My dad's old homemade boat with a tiller handle motor makes it so much fun.

After a quick run, dad idled back the motor and said, "throw em out!" That was the statement I was waiting for all morning. We were fishing for "specks" as we call them. I believe the species is commonly called the Speckled Perch. The approach we use is simple. Set the motor of the boat on the slowest speed possible and deploy as many different colored baits as possible. It's called "trolling" and allows you to cover a big area really fast rather than waiting for fish to come to you. You want to take note of which colors are catching the most fish and just start using that color for all of your baits. Like I said, it's a simple method. We made long parallel passes going back and forth for about twenty minutes.

The weather was holding up great and I fully expected the fish to start biting any time. We had baits out at varying distances behind the boat, so that some could run shallow and some could run deep. Dad would occasionally idle the motor a little faster also. We even reeled in the baits at one point to check for weeds. After another twenty minutes dad said, "okay, that's it. Reel 'em up, let's go home!"

I countered with, "let's give it another ten minutes," in my best optimistic voice.

He said nothing, just kept the motor at the same speed. Only a minute later as I was looking off in the distance at the beautiful cypress trees, I heard a commotion. I turned around to hear my dad shout, "fish on!" This was it, the turning point. Dad reeled in a nice speck and threw it in the cooler. We went back over the spot where he caught it several more times and nothing. We moved on and continued a grid-like pattern across the lake for another fifteen minutes. It was getting real clear that we weren't going to catch any more. I exclaimed, "well, we gave it a good try!" We reeled in the baits and headed back to the boat ramp.

That could have been it. We expected to catch fish but only caught one. We could have given up fishing altogether, *if* we would have given into being totally defeated after our high expectations. The next weekend we went fishing and almost caught the limit.

When we set our expectations high we run the risk of not achieving the goal we want. That's a risk I'm willing to take. The bigger the goal, the more action you take. The increased action produces more results. Learn from those results and take better action next time.

I set the goal pretty high when I went fishing with my dad. We had went fishing before with less than favorable conditions and did well putting fish in the cooler. Expectations are only our perceived vision of the future. Never let something that hasn't happened yet keep you from unleashing the leader within.

We tend to lean in the opposite direction when it comes to issues. We let our minds wander with all of the negative things that could happen. Leaders take into account the negative factors and choose to concentrate on the positive outcomes. Be sure to detail anything that is a deterrent to your goal but take all of the positivity you can get.

Be careful of your expectations. Hope for the best and plan for the worst.

HOW CAN I BETTER PLAN FOR WHEN MY EXPECTATIONS ARE NOT MET?

_____

_____

_____

_____

_____

_____

_____

_____

_____

_____

_____

_____

_____

_____

_____

_____

_____

_____

_____

_____

_____

_____

_____

CHAPTER 11

Leading The Way

Growing up my dad owned a heavy
equipment business digging ponds, lakes,
and dredging canals. Instead of spring break
from the ages of ten to thirteen, I went to
work. Don't get me wrong, it was work but
every job had to do with water. My birthday is
February 15th, the sign of Aquarius. I didn't
like the work so much but being able to swim
and fish was a nice perk. I had no idea I was
learning valuable skills that would serve me

well. I remember one time being on spring break and I was working with my dad. I was probably twelve or thirteen years old at the time.

We had a dredging job for the owner of a major automobile dealership. The job: make the lake deeper. No problem with a dredge like the one my dad had. It was like a big barge and floated on the water. This particular dredge would trolley on a cable back and forth. After a cut was made or all the material was removed from that section, we would simply move the cable over at both ends and start another cut. A dredge works in three ways. The first part is lowering the boom or "cutter head" down to the dirt, mud or whatever material you want to remove. The second thing a dredge does is create suction from a pump driven by an engine. Once that suction is created there has to be a discharge of that material somewhere. Of course there are a few more details but that's pretty much the basics.

Occasionally, the dredge would need maintenance or parts would need to be repaired. Of course, these "issues" were always in places that were almost impossible to reach or get to. It required taking what seemed like hundreds of nuts and bolts out of part after part to get to. Unless, of course, you were the smallest person around and could fit just about anywhere and just happened to be fairly handy with a wrench.

One day the pump needed an adjustment. It was a very simple "fix" that would probably take about five minutes to accomplish. The only problem was the cab (the place where the operator of the dredge sits) was positioned directly over the pump. It was big and heavy. Not to mention all the bolts holding it in place. As I took a small boat to the shore to get the necessary tools I started thinking to myself, "I'd rather be fishing."

That's when I got a genius idea. I could probably take a handful of wrenches and squeeze by the engine, shimmy under the cab and end up in a fairly good position when I reached the pump. When I reached the shoreline I stayed seated in the boat. I told my dad my plan and after some thought he agreed to give it a try. About fifteen minutes later I emerged from the depths of the dredge covered from head to toe in oil and grease but victorious. A job that would usually have taken over an hour had taken a quarter of the time.

I had taken the lead. I saw a problem and solved it. It was a win-win! The boss was back on schedule with the project and I was back to fishing. At the time this took place, you could say I was being quite selfish. My main goal was getting what I wanted but it just happened to speed things along and contribute to the goal, which was to get back to dredging.

There is one attribute great leaders are definitely not, and that is being selfish. Of course, there are goals to achieve, deadlines that have to be met, even dreams to accomplish. When we are selfish in any scenario it becomes a lose-lose proposition. The team or person feels taken advantage of, and while we may possibly feel the initial boost in confidence after achieving whatever it is we were striving for. The reality of despair and disappointment will set in sooner or later, taking any "win" we got out of it away.

A strong leader is one who in the face of adversity can solve a problem that ultimately leads to a "win-win" situation for all parties involved! Take the lead and lead the way. Get out in front of every situation and forge a path that everyone can follow.

We can use experiences we have had to come up with some great ideas. Whatever those ideas may be, make sure it is a win-win.

WHAT ACTION OR STEPS CAN I TAKE RIGHT NOW TO ENSURE A WIN-WIN ON MY CURRENT GOAL?

_____

_____

_____

_____

_____

_____

_____

_____

_____

_____

_____

_____

_____

_____

_____

_____

_____

_____

_____

_____

_____

CHAPTER 12

Understand Why Being Genuine is Attractive

Do you ever notice how when you first meet someone and within the first minute you've already made a decision if you like them or not? There are a multitude of factors that go into that decision. Some important factors may include the person's appearance, the sound of their voice, the way they make you feel. After only a few moments our mind takes in all this information, processes it, and reaches a conclusion. The old adage;

"Don't judge a book by its cover!"

really comes in to play here. Have you ever met someone for the first time and, as you continue talking with them, it occurs to you they may be fudging the truth about what they do or may have done just a little? Maybe even taking it over the top? This sometimes trips a switch that may make you think the person is dishonest or untrustworthy. It's really no secret that people just want to be liked, and an easy way to do that is to talk about themselves. Maybe it's a bit of insecurity that their story isn't "good enough" or "exciting enough" but it's still true that we all embellish sometimes. C'mon, like you've never stated on your resume that you were a "Communication Data Analyst" when in fact your position title was "Receptionist!"

In a previous chapter, we talked about how in conversations it's easy to get into a competition of trying to one-up somebody. Sure it's easy to fall into that trap. It's also super easy to just be *genuine.* An admirable quality all leaders should strive to attain. Oh, and it's super sexy too!

In 2004 an unprecedented three hurricanes crisscrossed the state of Florida, causing severe damage. At the time I was a project manager for a marine construction company. The coastline of Volusia County sustained massive erosion that caused many seawalls to fail. The condominiums and hotels that the seawalls protected were in immediate danger of falling into the ocean. The waves would generally be about one hundred yards from the seawalls and never come remotely close during calm conditions. This was a dramatically different scenario! Not only had the hurricanes damaged the seawalls but the constant thirty mile per hour northeast winds drove the waves into the walls nonstop. The already failing walls were pounded, and rocked back and forth. Eventually the concrete would break and the water would rush behind the wall, carrying the sand back out with it. I learned a valuable lesson during this experience;

"You can't fight mother nature!"

My company needed personnel and we needed them fast! When major events like this happen, all kinds of people come out of the woodwork looking to capitalize and make a quick buck. You can just imagine all of the people showing up wanting to be put to work. I needed heavy equipment operators to move and spread sand in the areas where the walls were broke. The water carried the sand away almost as fast as it would be put in place. We were buying time (extremely expensive time) so that we could get the new walls installed.

Generally, a new hire would go through the process of an application including a resume and would be scheduled for an interview. If the interview went well, we would go out to a project we were working on and have the applicant demonstrate their skills on a piece of equipment. In this case, there was absolutely no time for any of that. The first few people that showed up talked about all of their past jobs and explained they were the best for the job and that there was no reason to look any further. They had done this and that and had accomplished feats on an excavator that no other person in the world could ever do.

Having operated excavators for the better part of my life, I was a bit amused to say the least but there was no time to waste. I put them on the machines and gave them simple instructions that dump trucks would be arriving and all they had to do was keep pushing sand towards the seawall. I took off to another site where a wall was collapsing and needed attention fast. We had scheduled a couple of guys to meet with us at this location as well. I jumped out of the truck and found the waves had demolished about ten feet of the wall in front of the condo and had already eroded the sand. Just then a dump truck arrived with the first load of sand. I turned to the guys who had semi-frightened looks on their faces and asked them both a straight forward question. "Do you know how to operate that machine?" The first guy stated he was familiar with the machine but had never done anything like this before. I laughed as I told him, "now you can say you have!" I gave him a key to a machine and he went to work.

The other guy said, "honestly, I've never operated these kinds of machines but I'm willing to give it a try, if you'll give me the chance." At the time I was fresh out of options and needed to be three other places at one time. There was about to be a major loss of personal property if I didn't act quickly. I threw him the key and wished him luck.

It took only a minute to get back to the first location where I had the first two guys working. I pulled up to see three dump trucks waiting to unload and three piles of sand already on the ground. The two new operators were in panic mode trying to move too much sand at once and not really moving much at all. I stopped the first guy I came to and told him to start directing the dump trucks to unload one at a time. I jumped on the machine and in about fifteen minutes was able to get everything under control. I called my office to let them know I needed two more operators.

As it turned out, these two know-it-all, best-in-the-world operators could barely get the machines to move, much less move sand efficiently. I told them thanks for trying out but they were not exactly the right fit for our organization. I pushed a few more loads of sand behind the wall and had a large mound built up.

That's when I realized the emergency back in front of the other condo. I couldn't get there fast enough. I pulled into the parking lot to find the majority of sand moved to the place it was needed most. I just sat in my truck for a while and watched. The operators were working as a team with one of them pushing sand from the piles to the other one who would strategically place it where it was needed.

I remembered what the two guys had said when we had first met. They were both *genuine* in their answers. They were definitely not great operators but they were getting the job done.

The takeaway, start with yourself and just be honest and *genuine*! It's really easy and people find that as an attractive quality!

WHAT ACTION OR STEPS CAN I TAKE RIGHT NOW TO BE MORE GENUINE?

_____

_____

_____

_____

_____

_____

_____

_____

_____

_____

_____

_____

_____

_____

_____

_____

_____

_____

_____

_____

_____

CHAPTER 13

Urgency

Growing up in Emporia, Florida, I only knew of about seven families in the area. One of those families had a son about my age. I met him when I was about nine years old and I thought it was cool that he had a dog. A German Shepherd just like I had when I was younger. My dog Jake was my constant companion—he would walk in front of me and get between me and anyone else that tried to touch me.

My mom told me of a story about Jake's mom. His mom's name was Wendy and she would walk behind me down to the pond and grab my diaper when I got too close. My mom said I was fine as she watched from the kitchen window.

Thirty-five years ago, I learned that my friend Wendy had passed away. As of today, while I'm writing this, I am forty-six years old and I just cannot fathom the thought of wasting another minute. We work for the weekend, working forty plus hours per week just to enjoy two days off. What kind of life is this?

I'm reminded of the time when I was much younger—I lived in a house next to some neighbors and my grandparents lived around the corner. I was staying with my grandpa at the time and he wanted to go visit his friend next door. We took the car around the corner and pulled into his yard. We were there a while and I realized my favorite show ever was about to come on.

Of course it was "Gilligan's Island." I really loved that show, Gilligan was such a goof. I was playing in the yard when I wanted to go watch my show. I walked inside and couldn't find my grandpa anywhere so I just left, walked down the long driveway, and then all the way around to my grandma and grandpa's house. I sat down and watched the whole show. When it was over, I went outside in the yard and started to play again.

My grandpa came flying into the yard in that old Dodge Dart. He yelled at me to get over there. I could see he was really mad. I walked over to him cautiously. He picked me up by one hand and wore my bottom out with the other. He told me to never ever leave without telling someone again. That was more than likely the very first time I had experienced a sense of urgency not only on my part but my grandpa's part as well. I'm quite certain I got over it a lot quicker than my grandpa as he was still agitated the next day. I can only imagine his fear when he couldn't find me and the sense of urgency he had.

The kind of urgency of losing a loved one or not being able to find someone is not really what we're after at this point but you get the point. Living our lives with a slight sense of urgency can make remarkable differences on our outlook and outcomes.

Another time I'm reminded of is when my friend Chuck and I were out on my boat one day. We were on Lake George in central Florida having a great day. We had visited

Silver Glen Springs and went up into the spring Run of Juniper Springs. On our way out we both noticed that half the sky was a brilliant blue and the other half was as black as night. A huge storm was moving extremely fast in our direction and, as you probably know, a small boat on a big lake in a big storm can prove disastrous. Talk about a sense of urgency! We had to get cover and fast. When we came back into the lake, the waves were already reaching three to four feet and getting higher. The wind was picking up, blowing directly across the bow of the boat.

We could see the jetties and started heading that way. As soon as we got out into the lake we could see the storm a lot better. It was a lot worse than we had ever imagined. The jetties that you had to go through to enter into the St. John's from the lake was a no wake zone. I ignored every sign as I went just as fast as that boat would go. When we made it through the jetties, there was a Florida Wildlife Commission officer and his partner in a boat. They were waving their arms frantically telling us to stop. I backed off of the throttle and the boat eased down into the water.

They were hollering at us, "what do you think you are doing? That's a no wake zone!" I apologized to the officers and told them I was just trying to beat the storm back in. They told us to get out of there and don't ever let that happen again. I tried to crank the boat but we were out of gas. They quickly tied a rope to our boat and pulled us back into a nearby fish camp. Just then the bottom fell out of the sky and it rained so hard you couldn't even see across the river.

Having a slight sense of urgency can pay dividends in the long run. Not necessarily that dire urgency in the stories I shared with you, but enough urgency to get the job done. Some people know they have a deadline so they procrastinate and put things off until the last-minute. Leaders do not do this. They start a project as soon as they get it and do it with a slight sense of urgency. This will take the unneeded stress out of having your back to the wall when the deadline is up. Being assertive with yourself and others will help with this. Remember slow and steady wins the race when added with a slight sense of urgency.

WHAT CAN I DO TODAY TO CREATE A SLIGHTY HIGHER SENSE OF URGENCY?

_____

_____

_____

_____

_____

_____

_____

_____

_____

_____

_____

_____

_____

_____

_____

_____

_____

_____

_____

_____

_____

_____

CHAPTER 14

The One Sentence

What if there was a blueprint for success? Would you use it? I'm a huge fan of templates. You can search online and find templates for almost anything you can possibly imagine. The problems I've found with them are they're either too complex or really don't address the issue you want to resolve or the goal you want to meet. You can spend hours or even days writing out your plans or editing templates. All of these time-consuming activities are a big reason the majority of people never reach their goals. Remember the acronym KISS—*Keep It Super Simple*. I have developed a one sentence template where you can simply fill in the blanks to personalize your specific goal and create the blueprint to your success. Developing the one sentence template has taken me decades. I want to share with you the origins of its creation so you will have an understanding of its powerful qualities.

I've had the entrepreneurial spirit for as long as I can remember. I was reminded of this recently, while going through a box of old paperwork, I came across a script I had written when I was about ten years old. It said, "Wallace walks out of the ocean and up to the camera, holding a big Stringer of fish." Wallace says, 'I can catch a lot of fish and you can too!'"

I got a pretty big laugh out of it and was reminded that I never did complete that video. Back in those days there were no cell phones and the only video cameras available cost thousands of dollars. I tried just about everything I could but it never seemed to work out. The whole premise of my idea was to show a person how to make a chum bucket with wire mesh and a bucket. Turned out it was a great idea because there are millions of them sold today. I never followed through. I'm not really sure where I heard it or saw it but I learned even back then that every business should have a mission statement. At the top of that really old script it had in parentheses "Catch More Fish!" it was really solid and to the point.

I needed a template. Something short and quick to get aspiring leaders to take action. That's when I remembered that simple phrase "Catch More Fish!" It was to the point with no frills and that's just what I needed. I played with a paragraph for a while but it just seemed too much. Too much to remember, too much to read. I kept working on it, taking out the fluff words and getting down to the very basic sentence that could quite possibly be your blueprint to success. I've shared it in presentations and people have responded that it works.

I've heard and read many times that repeating a mantra or short phrase can immediately and overtime work in positive ways. Top athletes envision themselves already winning. They say things to themselves like, "I am a winner." I've developed this one sentence through many years of research and it includes the past, present, and future, making it the ultimate sentence. It can be used over and over again just by simply filling in the blanks.

Are you ready for it, here it is:

Even though _____ I will _____ by _____ !

I used this simple sentence to start my Brazilian Jiu-Jitsu Academy over four years ago. This is what I wrote down, (yes, you have to write it down)

Even though <u>I have no money</u> I will <u>start a Brazilian Jiu-Jitsu Academy</u> because <u>I have no other choice</u>!

Do you ever catch yourself making a mistake and say to yourself, "I'm such an idiot!" or something like that? Don't do that! You are tearing little holes in your self-esteem. Remember to watch your language, especially with yourself.

Go ahead and have fun with this one simple sentence. It can be used for practically anything. Be sure to post it on your bathroom mirror so you see it every morning. Post it on the dashboard of your car. Make it your mantra! Own it!

Whenever you get down on yourself or have a minor setback. Just read your mission statement. It's really simple but it works.

The beauty of this sentence statement is that you can use it again and again. Just change the words and you are off to the races again.

You can do it I promise. Unleash the leader within!

Here's The One Sentence again. ;

Even though _____ I will _____ by

_____!

_____

_____

_____

_____

_____

_____

_____

_____

_____

_____

_____

_____

_____

_____

_____

_____

_____

_____

_____

_____

_____

_____

_____

CHAPTER 15

The Key To Unleashing The Leader Within

As a child growing up in rural central Florida, I despised shoes. I went barefoot whenever possible. When I would get home from kindergarten, I would kick off my shoes as far as they would go. Not having any other kids around my age, I would let my imagination run wild as I played in the woods between our house and my grandparents'. I learned rather quickly that sandspurs not only hurt when you step on them but hurt just as bad when you have to pull them out. I remember one time when I was running back to my house, crossing the pasture and I learned what a fire weed was. I think the proper name is "stinging nettle." I didn't step on it which is quite painful. It actually went between my toes as I was running and my toes stripped the leaves clean off. I honestly thought my foot was going to catch on fire. If you grew up in the south you undoubtedly have a grimace on your face right about now and understandably so. Couple all of these diabolical foes with wasps and fire ants, and you'd think I'd be more open to wearing shoes, but unless it was mandatory by Mom, I was barefoot.

My grandma, affectionately called "Aunt Coot" by her friends, taught me all about the plants in her yard. She had little gardens all over her five acre property. She showed me how to care for them and how to start new plants from cuttings. I started a very short-lived little garden in my bedroom one time. I noticed the fire weeds in our yard had little white flowers on them and decided it would be a good idea to dig them up, put them in containers, and put them in my room. My mom obviously thought it was not a good idea and made me throw them out but my love of horticulture lived on.

My grandpa showed me how to graft orange trees by cutting small stems off one tree and splicing them onto another variety of orange tree to make one tree produce two kinds of fruit. Pretty cool! It's done by cutting a notch on one tree at a precise point and taking the cutting of another tree and securing it with fabric. If you keep the area moist it will bond and grow together. I learned to grow gardens with my grandparents and I was always in charge of the cucumbers and watermelons. As I got older I would check books out of the library (there was no such thing as the internet back then) and learn all I could about plants and how to grow them. I have since started and sold two landscape companies.

You may be asking yourself what in the world does all this has to do with the key to unleashing the leader within. The answer is fairly simple. I have been describing it all along. Have you figured it out yet? If not I'll keep the suspense building just a little longer. Just one more story.

The year was 2011, not long after the terrible terrorist attacks. I was working for an electric company installing conduits, electric cables, and giant transformers. The company had a contract with the largest electric provider in Florida. I loved my job. I got to drive a big crane truck and deliver all the materials needed for housing developments.

My friend was on one of the installation crews and he told me a story one day. He said he was on a job site installing the underground electrical pipes that needed to be buried at least thirty-six inches underground. He explained that his blueprint for the job matched the paint marks (showing other buried utilities) on the ground, but that all of the locations had been wiped out from a motor grader that had just been working in the area. He stated that he just kept digging with his backhoe machine and about forty-five minutes later, one of the guys in the trench that was laying the pipe held up two ends of some frayed wires. He said it was probably some old cable someone had buried long ago. Ten minutes later two white vans pulled up and the guys jumped out, telling him and his crew they had to evacuate.

He later found out that the frayed cable was the transcontinental fiber optic cable. Now I'm not sure if the story is entirely true but about a month later our whole office was given an ultimatum. Move to Bradenton Florida and keep working for the company or get laid off. I didn't much like the idea of leaving my family and friends so I took the pink slip and did what every normal person does. I signed up for scuba lessons.

After I graduated as an open water diver, I went right in to advanced dive school. I'm currently certified to dive to a depth of one hundred thirty five feet. Although I haven't done it in a while, I'm excited that several of my friends have recently become certified and I'm looking forward to many underwater adventures.

So what is the key to unleashing the leader within? Without any reservations I can tell you without a doubt that the key is <u>Constant Learning</u>! A leader is always looking to better themselves and in return sharing their knowledge with others. It's definitely not being a know it all! It's about gaining technical knowledge to make the team better.

It's all about giving, rather than receiving. Learn everything you can and become an expert in your field. Share your knowledge and unleash the leader within.

WHAT ACTION OR STEPS CAN I TAKE RIGHT NOW TO BE A SUBJECT MATTER EXPERT?

_____

_____

_____

_____

_____

_____

_____

_____

_____

_____

_____

_____

_____

_____

_____

_____

_____

_____

_____

_____

_____

_____

CHAPTER 16

Generally Speaking

We've already learned that listening to respond rather than reply is a great technique to build leadership skills. The same holds very true for the opposite and that is speaking.

I recently competed at the area level of the 2017 Toastmasters International Speech contest (based on the introduction to this book). It was exciting to win first place but what was even more exciting was when someone came up to me after the event and asked if I could give the same presentation for her high school. If that's not a confidence booster, I don't know what is. I commanded the stage that day after two amazing speakers. Sure, I was nervous but I was more confident than nervous. I put it all on the line and gave my best presentation of that speech I had ever given.

It wasn't always that way. Not by any means. When I was much younger, it wasn't that I didn't know what to say, but finding the right words to say was a huge problem. Getting my point across was difficult to say the least. In my early adulthood I was fortunate to be hired as a foreman, which meant talking to a group of people. In a previous chapter you found out how well that went. It was quite the learning experience. Flash forward up to seven years ago where I accepted a position as an Environmental Law Enforcement Officer. My job is to investigate complaints and knock on doors. When I first started that part of my career, my training officer told me, "know your job!" (you might want to write that down in your notes following this chapter) and handed me a folder full of County Ordinances and State

Statutes. I read everything twice and was able to quote the primary laws we enforce. By knowing my job I'm able to speak clearly and concisely with complainants and suspects. I also sprinkle in small talk to form a connection.

Speaking doesn't get easier, you just get better. Speaking to one person or many can be simple if you:

- Know your subject
- Make a connection
- Speak with passion

Knowing what you're talking about should really be self-explanatory. If you're ever in doubt, that is the perfect opportunity to ask questions. Those questions can be directed at finding something that you may have in common. By talking about similar interests you can form a personal connection. As I say in my International Speech;

"It's not necessarily the words that are said, but the way those words make you feel that has that impact!"

Speaking with passion will leave a lasting impression with anyone you speak with. Be it one person or an entire auditorium. Leaders use passion to send the message home! Remember that speaking isn't always the words that come out of your mouth but body language plays important role as well. Be sure to use gestures that go well with whatever it is that you're speaking about.

How did I become a better speaker and presenter? I practiced, of course, and I also joined Toastmasters International. There are clubs all over the world. I'm sure there is one near you. I encourage you to give it a try. Toastmasters is a supportive group where you follow a tried and true plan to become a better speaker and leader. You don't have to compete. As a matter of fact most people don't compete. It's just simply a fun way to improve themselves with like-minded people.

Generally speaking, and as a general rule of thumb, it's recommended when speaking to someone to make eye contact. You don't have to stare into their eyes. I find that looking at an eyebrow or the nose works rather well. It shows that you are paying attention and showing interest to what that person is saying. Another tip is not using big words. Not everyone's vocabulary may be as broad as yours. If someone gets caught up in something that you said, they will focus on it and your words will fall on deaf ears. Try to remember the acronym KISS. It stands for *Keep It Super Simple.* It can be used very effectively when giving directions for a task or job you need help with.

Last but certainly not least: making a personal connection can be done by asking great questions to find something in common. When it's determined that there is no connection, which is very uncommon but does happen, here's what to do. A simple touch on the arm or shoulder will do the trick. I find if something funny was said by either party and we're both laughing, it's the perfect opportunity to reach right out there and touch them. It makes a real personal connection and anchors the happy experience. Someone may not remember your name but they will definitely remember the experience.

Improved speaking in any situation has numerous benefits. From getting your point across to a friend, or stepping on stage in front of hundreds. Improve your speaking and unleash the leader within.

WHAT ACTION OR STEPS CAN I TAKE RIGHT NOW TO BE A BETTER SPEAKER AND COMMUNICATOR?

_____

_____

_____

_____

_____

_____

_____

_____

_____

_____

_____

_____

_____

_____

_____

_____

_____

_____

_____

_____

_____

_____

_____

_____

CHAPTER 17

Get the Facts

Never believe anything you hear and only half of what you see. That's a very practical phrase in my experience. Taking things at face value can get you into a lot of trouble. It's extremely important to get all of the facts before making a decision or taking any action.

I learned this firsthand when I began my career as an Environmental Law Enforcement Investigator. My first call after training was about some illegally dumped debris on an empty lot near a subdivision under construction. A lady had witnessed everything that happened. She even provided a tag number to our call center. I received the information by email and immediately drove over to the dumpster. When I arrived I put on gloves and went through the debris looking for more evidence. I found some crumpled up invoices and estimates for a local remodeling company.

I bagged and tagged the information and began looking up the tag number the witness had luckily been able to get. It came back as being registered to a late model truck and the owner just happened to be the same as the name I had found on the invoices and estimates. "Wow," I thought to myself. My first case is about to be open and shut. I was feeling pretty good at that moment. I wrote down the name and address of the person the vehicle was registered to and entered the address in my GPS. It turned out the address was only a few blocks away. It was close to lunchtime but I was really excited to wrap my first case up. As I pulled up to the address, I noticed a truck in the driveway that fit the description provided by the witness and it matched the tag registration.

As I pulled my truck over to the curb and got out, I noticed the name on the side of the truck also matched the information I had found in the illegally dumped debris. I thought I was really on a roll and this case was a slam dunk. I walked to the front door and knocked. A lady opened the door, took one look at me and immediately called a guy's name, and walked away leaving the door open. I kept thinking this just keeps getting better and better. A guy walked to the door and asked, "what's going on?" I identified myself and told him I wanted to know who owned the truck parked in the driveway. The guy explained that it was his truck and was looking puzzled. I told him to relax that I only had a few questions for him. He stated that I had the wrong guy.

At that time I had had enough and told him I was charging him with commercial illegal dumping and that it was a third degree felony in Florida. I told him to wait outside the door and don't move. I walked to my truck to start the paperwork when I heard him say, "wait! Hold on just a darn minute. I haven't dumped anything." I turned around and told him I had enough evidence and really didn't care what he had to say. He said "wait, when did this happen?" I told him I was done talking. He stood there with a weird look on his face. I opened my vehicle and grabbed my citation book. I turned to see him walking towards me. I told him to stop right there. He stopped and put his hands up about shoulder height. He said, "look, I run a professional business and I would never dump anything. Just when did this happen?" He had calmed down and I could sense some urgency in his voice. I told him the dumping occurred the day before about five o'clock in the afternoon. I explained I had a witness who saw his truck and even wrote down the tag number. I also explained I had found paperwork matching his company name in the debris that was dumped.

I finished by telling him there was no way he was getting out of it. He looked at me and began to smile. He said it wasn't him and could prove it. I told him I was all ears but it would have to be good. He said his wife had just given birth to their first child and he was at the hospital all day until eight o'clock in the evening the day before. Just then a lady walked out of the house with a newborn. She asked the guy if everything was all right. He said sure honey, and she walked back inside. I said wow, that is a good one. I asked if it wasn't him then who was it? He explained that he had let his friend borrow his truck and it still had some construction debris in the bed when he had gone to the hospital. He said he thought his friend had taken it to the dump.

I told him to get his friend on the phone. I spoke with his friend and he admitted to the whole thing. I was stunned, of course. I had all the evidence in the world that pointed directly at one person, or so I thought. That's why it is so very important to get all of the facts before taking action. If I had charged the wrong guy it would have been an enormously huge mistake on my part and the poor guy would have had to take it to court just to clear his innocence. Even worse, the guilty guy would have gotten away with it.

Trying to get things done too fast causes mistakes. Getting all of the facts may take a little while longer but will pay dividends in the long run. It truly pays to be patient and get the facts.

WHAT ACTION OR STEPS CAN I TAKE RIGHT NOW TO BE A BETTER INFORMED AND GET THE FACTS?

_____

_____

_____

_____

_____

_____

_____

_____

_____

_____

_____

_____

_____

_____

_____

_____

_____

_____

_____

_____

_____

_____

CHAPTER 18

The Three Amigos Framework

Just like the five people you spend the most time with can significantly impact your life, these three friends I want to introduce you to can and will change your whole world if implemented properly. They hang out together all the time and are key to unleashing the leader within. They work very well independently but when they are together they provide a framework for an almost unstoppable force. Who are they? The first Amigo is:

Integrity

Here is the definition of integrity: doing the right thing even if no one is looking. I strongly believe that anything that can be learned is a skill. Integrity is a behavior. It is something that we do and therefore it is a skill. A very valuable skill. Albert Einstein did many studies on behavior. He concluded that it takes eleven positive actions to overcome a negative action. In other words if you do something wrong you'll have to do the same thing eleven times the right way to correct the habit.

I learned very quickly from my parents and grandparents the difference between right and wrong. As I grew older, I learned the difference from my classmates at school, my teachers, and definitely the principal. My family provided the basis for which my integrity was built on, teaching me morals, manners, courtesy and religion. My classmates wouldn't let me get away with anything. It's like they were psychic or something. My teachers were not as critical.

My high school principal on the other hand was a no-nonsense disciplinarian. Back in those days when you were sent to the principal's office it meant only one thing: "The Paddle." It was wider than my behind and it had holes drilled in it so it would move through the air faster.

You also know the difference between right and wrong. The decision is yours and yours alone. Leaders choose to do the right thing even if no one is looking. Be a person of integrity.

Honesty

It goes without saying that being dishonest will not get you very far in life. Lying to a cop will land you in court. Lying to a judge is perjury and will land you in jail. Not to mention that if you tell one lie, you will invariably have to tell another one to cover it up, and then another and another. Pretty soon you won't be able to remember all of them. It just isn't worth it.

I recently attended an assertiveness training class. I took the same course years ago but I enjoyed it and the facilitator so much I wanted to do it again. I was reminded that being honest with someone without hurting their feelings not only greatly helps the other person but helps you as well. It gives the other person positive, corrective criticism while giving them something to work towards and allows them to grow. It also helps you from feeling regret by letting things build up. When you are honest and clear the air, it allows you to move on to more important productive things. You see, honesty and integrity go hand in hand. It's very difficult to do the wrong thing when no one is looking and be completely honest with yourself.

The other day I dropped something on the carpet in my living room. I had to clean it up so I found a can of carpet cleaner under the kitchen sink. I read the directions and they explained the sooner you removed the stain the better the results would be. It makes sense that if I were to let the stain soak in it would be there forever. The same can be said for being honest. Mistakes and accidents happen. They're just a part of life. Be honest! Own up to mistakes quickly. Get them out in the open. Do not allow the stain to set in. Honesty still is the best policy.

Courtesy

The third and final Amigo in the framework is
certainly not the least important. Not by any
means. Courtesy is a skill that is seriously
lacking more than ever. Just recently I was
walking out of a convenience store. As I
pushed the door open, I looked over my
shoulder to see if anyone was behind me.
There was, so I held the door open for them. I
was surprised when the lady stopped, looked
at me, and said, "thank you so much, that
rarely happens anymore!" I hold the door for
everyone. I'm courteous, it's what I do. What
surprised me was that the lady actually
stopped to genuinely thank me. I get a
thanks every now and then but this time was
different. Don't get me wrong. I don't hold
doors for the thanks. I hold doors because it
is the right thing to do, it's called common
courtesy which is not too common anymore.

Courtesy certainly plays a large part in a
leadership role. Let's use listening as we
covered in a previous chapter as an example.
It is courteous to wait until a person has
finished speaking before responding.

Putting all three of these Amigos together builds a framework on which true leadership is built.

WHAT ACTION OR STEPS CAN I TAKE RIGHT NOW TO USE THE THREE AMIGO'S?

CHAPTER 19

Change Your Language

Assertive Self-Talk System For Success

Being effective in anything you do in life requires communication. Whether it's with your parents, teachers, boss, or a loved one. How you communicate will ultimately determine your outcome.

When you were a young child the world seemed limitless and you explored everything you possibly could. You had no idea what could hurt you but your parents did. They probably told you, "stop it! You can't do that! Don't do that!" Of course it was for your own good, to protect you. It also planted seeds that grow into negative self-Talk.

At my Brazilian Jiu-Jitsu Academy the word *can't* is not allowed. Not even in conversation. It forces kids and adults to search for other more positive words like *I'll try*. Changing this one simple word may seem insignificant but it actually has the potential to dramatically affect the outcome of nearly any situation. If one simple word can do so much, just imagine what several words can do!

"Whether you think you can or you think you can't, you're right!"

The rules to being an effective leader have certainly changed and the language we use with ourselves and others are the essential prerequisites of top performance. As a kid I learned to operate heavy equipment while working with my dad. I was probably about nine years old when I first operated a bulldozer. After a brief tutorial on all the levers and pedals, my dad cranked the machine up and said, "you can do it, take it slow." I was slightly scared and it's safe to say my anxiety level was through the roof. I wanted to learn and do a great job for my dad. It was difficult at first. I was all of three and a half foot tall at the time, and in order to work the throttle and the blade at the same time, I'd have to sit down. If I sat down, I couldn't see over the hood so I'd stand up and look where I was going, sit back down and adjust the blade. Steering had its own challenges. The bulldozer turned by stepping on a brake and pulling a big handle to turn left or right. I accomplished this by standing on the brake with both feet and pulling with everything I had on the lever. Up and down, up and down.

With lots of experience I learned to operate all kinds of heavy equipment. I became a foreman with all this experience I and worked for an underground utility company. I knew a lot about underground utilities but I was certainly not a leader. I was the boss and I made sure everyone knew it. I would bark orders and everyone would jump. Show up one minute late and you would get a harsh talking to. Yes, I was *that* boss! The one you wouldn't wish on your worst enemy.

It takes a crew of about five people to install underground storm drains. One person on an excavator to dig a trench, one person on a loader to bring a new section of pipe, a "hill" person to hook up that pipe, and a lead and tail man in the trench to ensure the pipe is on grade and connected to the previous pipe correctly. All of these people play an important role in an efficient crew. When one of those people aren't there, the foreman has to take up the slack and do their job. With a boss like I was, people would quit without warning or get fired for various reasons. It soon became crystal clear that even though I knew how to do everything, it simply wasn't physically possible to do everything. I realized I had to learn to be more patient. I learned rather quickly that being the "boss" was something totally different than what I thought it was.

How did I change things? What did I start to do differently? It was a very simple switch in the language I used. Not only the language I used in talking with the crew, but the words I used in talking to myself. Instead of getting upset because the project was not getting done fast enough that day and telling myself, "these guys are the slowest people ever," I started asking myself, "what can I do to help these guys?"

One day we were doing the same thing we did every other day and it just seemed to me the guys were bored. I walked over and told everyone to take a break. I told them a joke and everyone laughed. To my surprise, a minute later they all went back to work without being told. They had a little pep in their step too. I found that working together as part of a team paid much higher dividends than being a "boss." I began using positive self-talk with myself which turned into positive talk with the crew. I started using words like "we" instead of "you" and "let's try" instead of "just get it done." I started to feel a lot better about myself and the crew started performing like a well-oiled machine. To be an exceptional leader we must develop positive self-talk. We must begin with ourselves before taking on a team. The old adage,

"Sticks and stones may break my bones but words will never hurt me."

is very true! It's not the words but rather how those words make us feel that make an impact. The great news is we have the ability to change the words we use to communicate with ourselves and others. Start with excluding the word "can't" from your vocabulary. Replace it with the phrase, "I'll try." Yes, they're just words but the feelings and emotions we give those words will have dramatic impact on our relationships and ultimately our lives.

Let's get started with the Assertive Self-Talk System. As I talked about in the beginning of this book, I had severe anxiety. My grandpa explained that there was a power inside me that I had to unleash. That power was confidence. It all started with;

The most important conversation you will have is with yourself.

Step number one in the system begins with your self-image. How you see yourself is the basis for how you communicate with yourself and others. It all starts with the story you tell yourself. This creates your reality, your whole world and the best part is it's entirely up to you to create it. No matter what happens in life, you and only you determine exactly how to handle it by the story you tell yourself. You can decide the outcome of any situation. We can build a positive self-image with a simple exercise I call "Your Highlight Reel." This is designed to help you recall all of your life's achievements and start your assertive self-talk to true success.

Exercise #1

Make a list of your life's accomplishments. Start with your earliest known memory and be sure to include every accomplishment no matter how small.

_____

_____

_____

_____

_____

_____

_____

_____

_____

_____

_____

_____

_____

The next step—and this is extremely important—is to make copies of the list and put them where you will see them. It is constant reinforcement of a positive self-image.

"You are not successful today not by who you are but by who you aren't."

Exercise #2

Now it's time to let your mind run wild. I mean take it to the extreme. I want to know your wildest dreams. What do you want? Where do you want to go? Who do you want to be? What do you want to have? What will be your life's full potential? Make a list. I mean go crazy, listing everything you could possibly imagine having.

_____
_____
_____
_____
_____
_____

Congratulations! You have just organized your thoughts. You now know where you have been and where you are going.

We have thousands of thoughts every day. Most of them come in the form of self-talk. How you talk to yourself, the conversation you have is important for your confidence and self-esteem, but it is often overlooked. Self-talk is a soundtrack. The movie constantly playing in the background in your head. It's impact is dramatic. The conversations you have with yourself help determine your emotions and actions. Think about this for a minute. If you are constantly beating yourself up, how can you expect to feel good about yourself or believe in yourself?

Negative Self-Talk

Don't underestimate the great power of negative self-talk. If you are consistently reinforcing low opinions of yourself, you'll come to believe them and act as if they're real. You may not even be aware of the full extent of your negative self-talk, but when you're empowered with a little knowledge you can make some really positive changes.

The following points will help you to learn about the different types of self-talk and how to use them to your advantage.

Self-Talk in General

Self-talk is so natural that you may not even realize what you've been saying to yourself all of these years. If you want to make some positive changes in your life, you will need to become aware of the full extent of the problem before you can go about changing it.

The first step is to become conscious of the commentary you create about your life. Whenever you find yourself in a negative mood, pay attention to the things that you are saying to yourself and how they make you feel. You will soon begin to realize the level of damage that you are doing to yourself.

Exercise #3

Think of the negative phrases you tell yourself when things don't go your way. If you make a mistake, what exactly are the words you use? Make a list of these words now.

_____
_____
_____
_____
_____
_____
_____
_____
_____
_____
_____
_____
_____
_____
_____
_____
_____
_____
_____
_____
_____
_____
_____

Refer back to this list often. Make a point to remove or change these negative words. It will take time to totally delete these words from your self-talk. They have become habits over a long period of time. Take it slow but be deliberate.

Disrupt old patterns!

Just because you're saying it, doesn't mean that it is true. Do not be afraid to dispute your self-talk (yes, you can have a little argument with yourself). Challenge the harsh criticism by telling yourself out loud that those comments are untrue and you are over reacting.

Self-talk is an amazing tool for making changes. If you are beating yourself up about a lack of knowledge or skill, you can use this as an opportunity to create a learning plan for yourself and improve your knowledge and skillset.

Note: I strongly suggest that you look at every problem as an opportunity to learn and better yourself. With new skills come more confidence. Be a problem solver!

Conduct a reality check

Ask yourself how your self-talk measures up to what's really happening around you. Is there really a big difference between burning one slice of toast and being a failure in the kitchen?

Disruption is a powerful tool! You absolutely do not have to accept what you say in your self-talk. Be sure to challenge any negative thoughts. Utilize the list you made in exercise number three. You don't have to force yourself to be optimistic about everything, but you must avoid undue negativity.

Be consistent!

If you are negative with your self-talk, it didn't happen overnight. You've been telling yourself the same negative messages over and over again until you accepted the words as true. That is the power of consistency. The good thing is that you can use consistency to your advantage too. The more you focus on the words you say to yourself, the more you will recognize the negative self-talk and be ready to switch it quicker.

In exercise number one, we learned everything we have achieved by our current self-talk. In exercise number two we learned exactly where we want to go and what we want to have. We cannot get what we don't have by continuing doing what we have always done.

You don't have to live with negative self-talk. It doesn't have to be something which just happens. If you leave your negative self-talk unchallenged, the consequences will continue to get worse, to the point where they cripple your self-belief and self-esteem. Instead, you can channel your self-talk and start moving in a positive direction. Get in touch with the thoughts that automatically run through your head, and turn them into a steady stream of encouragement. You'll reduce stress, enhance your self-confidence, and enjoy more success in life.

Visualize success!

Picture yourself getting the results you want. Self-talk doesn't always take the form of words. The images and movies that play in your mind also deliver either a positive or negative message. When you focus on a positive image or scenario (i.e. achieving your goals) you are reminding yourself that you can do it, that you have the knowledge, skills, and attributes necessary to be successful in achieving those goals.

Positive visualization is one of the most powerful self-talk habits that you can practice. They say that a picture paints a thousand words, so make sure that you are focusing on positive, empowering imagery.

Look on the bright side!

Self-talk won't make life's challenges disappear. Bad things happen and if you want to continue to grow and thrive, you'll need to take on bigger and bigger challenges. There will be times when you have doubts and difficulties but these are opportunities to advance yourself. Remember, problems are only opportunities. Be a problem solver.

Instead of criticizing yourself for a past misstep, it's extremely important to concentrate on what you can do better in the future. It enables you to realize that you're a fallible human being. You understand that just as you have the ability to create some difficult moments for yourself, you can also create the life you want with the knowledge, skills, and attributes to overcome them and learn from your experience.

Exercise #4

In this final exercise we are going to refer to exercise number one. Review your list of accomplishments and choose the positive words that each accomplishment makes you feel. If you won an award you could choose "triumphant" for example. Make a list of these words and use them instead of the words you listed in exercise number three. Cross reference them at the end of the day and you will see, hear, and feel a difference in your life.

_____
_____
_____
_____
_____
_____
_____
_____
_____
_____
_____
_____
_____
_____
_____
_____
_____
_____
_____
_____
_____
_____

Congratulations!

You have completed the **Assertive Self-Talk system for Success**. Nothing you have learned will do you any good without taking action and implementing the strategies that were outlined. You are the leader of your life. It is up to you *and only you* to create the life you desire. Circumstances and people have absolutely nothing to do with your success. Everything has to do with how you act or react to any situation. It all starts with the story you tell yourself. Make it a good one!

To receive your **Certificate Of Completion**, please fill out the form.

Name_____

Email_____

What's your biggest take away from this course?

_____

_____

_____

_____

Would you recommend this course to a friend?

If yes, what is their name?

Ready to take it to the next level? Do you want to implement the strategies in this system and need a little help? Top athletes, top business people, and top performers have something in common. They all have a coach. Someone who has been there, done that, and has made all of the mistakes. Someone who has already learned how to succeed and is willing to share that knowledge. A mentor or coach will take you farther in your pursuit of success in a shorter amount of time. You can learn everything on your own but it will take trial and error and years to learn. Or you can partner with a mentor or coach and get where you want to go in less time.

Coach Wallace wants to partner with you. Visit;

https://www.coachwallace.com/coaching/

CHAPTER 20

Summary

Doing The Work

Read every book ever published. Watch every video on your chosen subject. Take advice from all of your friends. None of that information will have any impact on your life whatsoever.

Confidence

Everything you do leads to a result. The more you do, the more results you will have. The more chances you take, the more opportunities you will have. Use those experiences as learning opportunities. One of the all-time greatest NBA stars missed more shots than he made. Michael Jordan also attempted more shots than a lot of other players. Confidence is the underlying base for anyone that has had success in anything. Take the shot! Use every success you've ever had and build on it. Use that confidence to take another chance. You will find yourself living the life of your dreams.

Attitude

It's not what happens to us but rather how we choose to respond that makes the difference. Your attitude is extremely important. There will be issues. There will be trials. There will always be something that irritates you or makes you upset. It's just going to happen. Looking at issues from a different angle or point of view can make all the difference in the world. Look for the positive in any situation. If you find you made a mistake you can chock it up to a learning experience. Be a good finder, not a fault finder. No one likes the person always going around criticizing everything. It's not all rainbows, unicorns and snowflakes out there! Do your business. Get the job done but do it with gratitude and cheer.

Grow through life!

As kids we go to school. Some of us go to college. After school we get a job. It is so important to continue to educate ourselves throughout our lives, most importantly after the official education system. As we grow older our passions change. The difference in an average life and the extraordinary life is constant learning. Be it for the workplace, your business, or your passion. We need equal parts challenges (work) and relaxation. An amazing quote states;

"If you do something you love, you will never work a day in your life!"

I am a subscriber to this theory. I have a passion for sharing strategies with people so they can achieve their true potential. I had a passion so strong I set out to start a Brazilian Jiu-Jitsu Academy with a five hundred dollar credit card. I saw the potential to change people's lives through martial arts. Four years ago, I made that dream possible with one thing. A burning desire! I was determined to succeed. I didn't give up! I learned something new after every phone call, after every meeting, after every, "No!"

In only three months I opened my academy. I love my Gator Family! Four years later and we're going strong. I'm continuing to learn new things every day. How to provide exceptional service, how to market, how to build relationships. Be consistent in your quest for knowledge. Knowledge is power!

Lasting Change

Believing in yourself will not only keep you motivated but creates the willpower to change the world. You are the creator of your entire world. Make it a great one.

Being absolutely one hundred percent committed to each individual goal is crucial for lasting change. I sincerely hope you never have to go in for surgery. If you did, would you want the surgeon to come in the operating room talking about how he was partying to two o'clock in the morning?

Would that be okay with you? Surgeons have one goal. To save your life and make you better. I am suggesting that you hold yourself to the same standard. Save your life and make it better. Be one hundred percent committed to your passions, to your work, to your family.

Start with one thing!

Start with only one thing. Life can become overwhelming for sure. It all builds up into a sea of things to do. It can seem like a never-ending task with mountains of issues! Start with one thing. Make it your only goal. See it through. Sure, it will be hard but you're a problem solver. You are confident. You can do it, I promise, just unleash the leader within! In a world of constant bombardment of commercials on TV, Facebook, Instagram, and Google it's seriously surprising that we get anything done at all. The world has become infatuated with the Internet and social media. The drama has been taken to the next level. Focusing on one single thing will allow you the opportunity to realistically complete small tasks and boost your overall productivity.

That little voice!

I am convinced that the key to leadership is the conversation you have with yourself. Focusing on your accomplishments and learning from your mistakes will take you to the next level. I am reminded of a great quote that doesn't immediately make sense.

"If your goal doesn't scare you, it's not big enough!"

Dream big! Reach for the stars and you will achieve your true potential!

Focus on what matters most!

What's the biggest thing in your life? What does your mind go to every second of every day? Is it your family, your job, your passion? It is essential to prioritize what is most important to you. Create unique goals for yourself and see them through. Create small wins and use the momentum to be the best you can be. People can tell you what to do but it's up to you to deliver. Give people what they want and more. Think of it as investing in your future. People put money in the stock market as an investment. The more you put stock in people, the higher return you'll get.

> *"It's not what you know, it's who you know!"*

The one thing all leaders use to their advantage

Remember to listen to respond rather than react. It's not what happens to us but rather how we choose to respond that makes the crucial difference. I remember being in school and the teacher telling everyone before a test that a portion of the grade was based on writing your name on the top of the page. I have no idea why that stuck with me but it did. It helps me to remember now to follow directions. Try to listen to what people are really saying. Read between the lines so to speak. Observe their body language and put it all together. Leaders have a remarkable ability to gain incredible insight just by listening.

The blame game

Taking absolute, full responsibility of your thoughts and actions is the only way to take the lead. Any waiver toward blaming people or circumstances will cause multiple side effects. Keep in mind that you will always have to answer to yourself. One blame will turn in to another. Promise yourself that you will not play the blame gamc.

Taking personal responsibility

Being personally responsible means doing the right thing even though you may have to face some consequences. When I make a mistake, I'm the very first one to admit it. I take personal responsibility and own up to it immediately. The problems in the future would be far worse to overcome if I didn't. If things are not going my way, I look for ways to change it. This is your life. Own it!

Expectations

For many years of my life I did the same

thing over and over, and fully expected things to change one day. I learned that the only thing that stays the same is change. You just have to embrace change and go with the flow. Fighting change will make things in every situation more challenging and difficult than they need to be. With that being said, it is also very important to challenge the status quo. "Normal" is just a matter of opinion. If you want something different than you have, you will have to do something different than you have been doing. Go after what you want. Playing it safe will get you what you have already got. As the saying goes:

"Expect the best but plan for the worst!"

Leading the way

Be a game changer. Think way, way outside the box. In the early eighties every convenience store I walked into had pet rocks for sale. Seriously, it was an ordinary rock with a strip of fluffy hair and two boggle eyes. The inventor of the pet rock went on to be a millionaire. He had an idea, took a chance, and followed through. More times than not people told that guy it was a dumb idea. What's your idea? How can you change the world? What mark will you make? What will be your legacy? You are the designer of your world. Make it great!

Learn how being genuine is attractive

Just be yourself. Something that really hit home with me was something someone once told me.

"Don't compare your life to someone else's highlight reel!"

Think about that! We are addicted to social media. We have an app for everything. We go on sites and see everyone else's big wins and accomplishments. Occasionally we see setbacks, but for the most part we see everyone else's highlight reels on social media. It doesn't matter. It really doesn't. Just be yourself and do what you do. You can have so much more impact by being you than trying to be someone you're not. Be genuine. It's sexy!

Urgency

Patience is a virtue but there is only so much one should put up with. Life has no expectancy. To be perfectly honest, life is short. The current life expectancy is between sixty-eight years old and seventy-one years old. I heard this when I was a kid but as I grew older, I learned this quote to be perfectly true.

"The older you get, the faster time flies!"

Make a plan. A big plan. Stick to it. If someone offers you an opportunity that sounds great, do your research first. If it looks good, say yes and figure it out as you go. Never ever let fear stand in the way of your dreams. Try not to go so fast that you make mistakes but always remember that time is of the essence. Tomorrow is not promised.

The One Sentence

Through years of research and trial and

error, I've determined that this is the one sentence template that can be your blueprint to success. Be sure to go back to the end of the chapter and write as many sentences as you like. It can be used in so many ways and for so many goals. Write out a slip of paper or print one of your current sentence and keep it with you. Look at it and read it regularly.

The Key To Unleashing The Leader Within

Constant learning will keep your mind sharp and allow you to achieve your true potential. When Elon Musk and Bill Gates started their empires, do you think they knew how to do what they do now? Absolutely not. They had a vision, an idea. They took action and learned from the results. Their results speak for themselves. Constant learning does not have to be academics such as getting a degree. It is simply having an open mind and learning from different sources. A coach can help you dramatically increase your knowledge in a short amount of time. If coaching is not for you I'd like to suggest reading books or listening to podcasts on your subject of interest. Whatever you choose to learn from, just keep going. Be better than you were yesterday.

Generally Speaking

Your communication with others especially in a leadership role is crucial. Being able to get your point across in a clear and concise way will be the turning point in all relationships. If you can talk the talk, you'll take your achievements to a whole new level. Pay close attention to the words you use. Be considerate yet assertive.

Get The Facts

There is nothing worse than jumping to conclusions. It's extremely important to take into all accounts of every situation. You only have one chance to get it right. Get it wrong and the facts will come back to haunt you. Just be patient and put out facts. That's what my department does. We enforce the contract between the County and the County's contracted garbage company. Occasionally the resident has placed debris curbside on the County right of way that is out of compliance and we educate the resident. Sometimes there are discrepancies and it is extremely important to get and document all of the facts to achieve a resolution.

Take this analogy and apply it to your life. Make a contract with yourself. Include certain rules you must adhere to and enforce them. You are the architect of your own life! Always remember that you and only you have the power to change it.

The Three Amigos Framework

Integrity, honesty, and courtesy are powerful characteristics of leaders, each having their own unique benefits. When used together, these characteristics and skills can change lives. I say skills because each one can be learned. Use constant learning to build up your integrity. Be honest with yourself and others. Be courteous to everyone, especially when they don't deserve it. Your character depends on it.

Change Your Language

In my opinion, the story you tell yourself creates your entire reality. It's so very important to focus on the conversations that go on in our minds. Pay close attention to self-imposed limiting beliefs. Challenge your beliefs often to see if they really are true or not. Stay positive, you can do it, I promise! Just Unleash The Leader Within!

ABOUT THE AUTHOR

Wallace Bailey is an author, professional speaker, and leadership coach. He's also the Owner/Instructor at Gator Family Brazilian Jiu-Jitsu. In his first book, *Beyond Yesterday*, strategies to leave the past where it belongs, he explains techniques to move past your fears and struggles to finally live an extraordinary life. He presents Keynote speeches and workshops nationwide. Wallace continues to live in central Florida with his wife LeeAnn, dog Katie, and cat Lil' Mama. Wallace would love to connect with you.

For speaking engagements and coaching please visit;
www.coachwallace.com

or by email
talktome@coachwallace.com

UNLEASH THE LEADER WITHIN
ACHIEVE YOU TRUE POTENTIAL